BLESSED
CARLO
ACUTIS

5 steps to being a saint

Mgr Anthony Figueiredo, STD

All booklets are p...
thanks to the generosity ...
of the Catholic Tru...

Contents

Everyone is born as an original, but many people end up dying as photocopies.

Preface

"Did you know Carlo Acutis?" I heard this question asked many times during the amazing days of his beatification in Assisi. I had to answer: unfortunately, no. When I arrived in Assisi, as bishop, in February 2006, we were in the winter months during which Carlo was in Milan. In the summer, he returned to the city of Saint Francis, as he was used to doing with his family, but I never had occasion to meet him. By October, his earthly life was already on track to heaven.

Nevertheless, I do like to note that, in reality, this is not quite true. Antonia, Carlo's mother, reminded me that in the previous year, in Rome, Carlo and I had met, but without my realising it. I was then secretary of the Congregation for Divine Worship. On 5th May, 2005, I participated in a Congress on eucharistic miracles held at the Athenaeum Regina Apostolorum. On that occasion, the Exhibition of Eucharistic Miracles, designed by Carlo, was also on display, and he was there. We may have greeted each other in passing. I would never have imagined that fifteen years later, I would witness his beatification.

That encounter, which vanished from my memory, has taken on for me the value of a message. It reminds me of an aspect of holiness: the saints do not point to themselves, but to God. They do not exhibit their face, but the face of Jesus. The secret to their holiness is precisely this "losing themselves" in Jesus. By becoming one with him, the light of Jesus shines on their face, makes it glow, and attracts.

This explains the tens of thousands of people who, between 1st and 19th October 2020, streamed to Assisi to venerate the mortal remains of Carlo, exposed in the Sanctuary of the Renunciation. The face of this boy of our time, full of life and dreams, but, above all, full of Jesus, touched the heart. It has given a breath of hope at a time when the pandemic is saddening the world. Most especially, he has made us remember that holiness is possible at any age and in any state of life. We are all called to it.

Carlo now makes this invitation to holiness in tandem with Francis of Assisi, in the Sanctuary that recalls the place where the young son of Bernardone, eight hundred years ago, stripped himself of all his earthly goods, to be fully God's and to give himself entirely to his brothers and sisters. At the entrance to the Sanctuary, a painting depicts them together, pointing to Jesus, inviting pilgrims to enter first of all for the celebration and Eucharistic Adoration. The Lord comes first, then the saints. They are only witnesses, given to us as intercessors and models of life.

I thank Monsignor Anthony Figueiredo for this truly beautiful, agile, and inspiring book. It is historically well documented. It is theologically profound. Here he offers us not only a biographical profile, but a "road map" of holiness in the footsteps of Carlo. We are not all called to the charismatic choices of Francis of Assisi, but we can all follow the simple way of Carlo. It takes nothing away of what makes life beautiful, but everything hinges on Jesus, in particular on the Eucharist, the "highway to heaven."

Carlo Acutis is an invitation. An invitation addressed to everyone, especially the young, not to waste life, but rather to make of it a masterpiece. Only God makes us capable of this. "Not I, but God": this is the winning formula of the young Blessed. The only formula – to quote his own words – that makes us "original," and not "photocopies."

✠ DOMENICO SORRENTINO,
Bishop of Assisi
Assisi, 26th October 2020

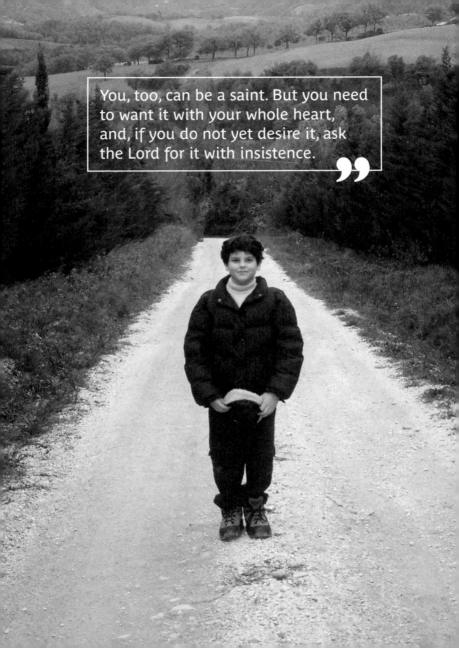

You, too, can be a saint. But you need to want it with your whole heart, and, if you do not yet desire it, ask the Lord for it with insistence.

Opening Reflections

How remarkable it is that, from such a young age, the desire of Carlo Acutis for himself and others was that we become saints! His short yet intense life of just fifteen years, spanning two centuries and crossing the threshold of the second millennium, shows how he fulfilled this desire for himself, and how he has provided a road map to holiness in our times for us all and for young people especially.

The French novelist, Léon Bloy, writes: "The only real sadness, the only real failure, the only great tragedy in life, is not to become a saint." This is the unwavering call that the Church makes to all people throughout the ages. It comes from Jesus himself, who ends his most important and longest of teachings – the Sermon on the Mount – with the call to his disciples to "Be perfect, as your heavenly Father is perfect" (*Mt* 5:48). Through his Paschal Mystery – his suffering, death, resurrection and ascension – Jesus gives us the grace to be perfect through the outpouring of the Holy Spirit. In the centuries that followed, the Fathers of the Church repeatedly called Christians to holiness, as did the Councils of the Church. In its "Universal Call to Holiness in the Church" (Chapter V of the Dogmatic Constitution *Lumen gentium*), the Second Vatican Council states,

All the faithful of Christ of whatever rank or status, are called to the fulness of Christian life and to the perfection of charity … In order to reach this perfection, the faithful should use the strength dealt out to them by Christ's gift, so that … doing the will of the Father in everything, they may wholeheartedly devote themselves to the glory of God and to the service of their neighbour. (n.40§2)

Pope St John Paul II, who raised to the altar more saints than any of his predecessors, refers to holiness as "the prime and fundamental vocation" that God the Father assigns to each of us. "Holiness is the greatest testimony of the dignity conferred on a disciple of Christ" (Post-Synodal Apostolic Exhortation *Christifideles laici*, n.16). No one is excluded from offering this testimony, not even the young; as St John Paul II prophesied in 1994: "There will be saints and apostles among children!" Pope Emeritus Benedict XVI challenges young people to "dare to be glowing saints, in whose eyes and hearts the love of Christ beams." In our own times, Pope Francis has offered compelling words on the call to holiness in his Apostolic Exhortation *Gaudete et exsultate*, dedicated entirely to the theme of holiness

> Holiness is not the process of adding, but subtracting: less of me to leave space for God.

in today's world: "The Lord asks everything of us, and in return he offers us true life, the happiness for which we were created. He wants us to be saints and not to settle for a bland and mediocre existence" (n.1).

From the beginning, the message is clear. We are called to be saints. Countless holy persons over the ages have attested to this. "God would never inspire me with desires that cannot be realised," St Thérèse of Lisieux writes, "so in spite of my littleness, I can hope to be a saint." But, looking at ourselves – our weaknesses, failures and sins – we might well ask, how? That was the question that I put to the saintly Mother Teresa of Calcutta as a newly ordained priest: "If you have the desire to be holy, Father," she replied, "God will do the rest."

"The only thing we have to ask God for, in prayer," Carlo would say, "is the desire to be holy." In most ways, he was a boy like any other of his age. Yet he did not fall into the temptation of so many others, who wanted to be different, but followed the crowd. As a result, Carlo said, "Everyone is born as an original, but many people end up dying as photocopies." In imitation of the words of St Catherine of Siena – "Be who God meant you to be and you will set the world on fire" – he nurtured his desire to be a saint. He loved the Church and availed himself of the grace of the sacraments. He entrusted himself to the Blessed Mother and followed in the footsteps of holy men and women. He had a heart for the poor. He used his great talents with the internet for the good of souls. Thus he was able to end his days, saying: "I am happy to die because I have lived my life without wasting a minute on those things which do not please God."

Do you and I wish the same – for ourselves, our children, those we teach or catechise? Do you and I have the desire to be holy? If so, the life of Blessed Carlo Acutis, the first millennial Blessed, shows us a simple road map to holiness, by following five practices, accessible to us all, that we can count on the fingers of one hand. I invite you to read on.

CHAPTER ONE

The Beginnings: Normal and Holy

Carlo's earthly journey began in London on 3rd May 1991. His partly English father, Andrea Acutis, and Italian mother, Antonia Salzana, had business ventures in London and lived at 4 Gledhow Gardens, SW5. The Acutis family were, and still are, owners of a large insurance company, Vittoria Assicurazioni S.p.A. On 18th May, 1991, Carlo began his life as a child of God through the sacrament of Baptism at the Church of Our Lady of Dolours on Fulham Road in the Borough of Kensington and Chelsea in London, a parish run by the Servite Order (the Servants of Mary) and dedicated to Our Lady of Fatima. He was given the name Carlo Maria Antonio. "Carlo" because that was his grandfather's name. Yet, from that moment, St Charles Borromeo, the holy Archbishop of Milan, became his protector and patron. As he grew up, Carlo developed a special love for the Virgin Mary and St Anthony of Padua. Both sets of grandparents came for the Baptism of the first-born child, as did Carlo's great grandmother, Adriana. His godparents were his grandfather, Carlo Acutis, and his maternal grandmother, Luana.

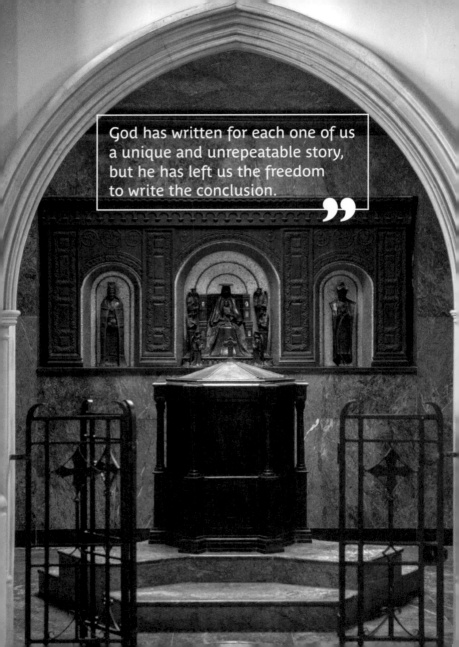

God has written for each one of us
a unique and unrepeatable story,
but he has left us the freedom
to write the conclusion.

The importance of this moment and Carlo's parents bringing their child to Baptism cannot be overemphasised, especially in light of what was to unfold in this boy's short life. The Catechism of the Catholic Church teaches that sanctifying grace, received in Baptism, "perfects the soul itself to enable it to live with God, to act by his love" (n.2000). Carlo's parents were nominal Catholics, attending Mass rarely. His mother admits that, coming from a non-practising family, before Carlo she had been to Mass only for her First Communion, her Confirmation and her wedding. "I was not the ideal model of a Catholic mother," she says. His father's faith was lukewarm. When the two dated, neither went to Church. Carlo's parents might well have chosen not to baptise their son or to leave the choice to him in his adult life. It would have meant to deprive God of his power to act through the sanctifying grace bestowed in Baptism.

Years later, Carlo himself recognised the fundamental importance of the sacrament – the gateway to life in the Spirit – that he had received:

> Baptism allows souls to be saved thanks to the readmission to Divine Life. People do not realise what an infinite gift it is, and, apart from thinking about giving sweets and the white garment, are not worried at all about understanding the meaning of this great gift that God gives to humanity.

Again, let us reflect on the possibility that Carlo, who died at the age of fifteen, might have not been baptised or might have been left the choice to decide later.

The Acutis family returned home to Milan in September 1991. In most ways, Carlo was a perfectly normal child growing up. At the age of four, he began pre-school, which he enjoyed immensely, since he liked being with other children. His summers were spent with his maternal grandparents in Centola, a town in the southern region of Campania. Here, he immersed himself in the beauty of the sea and nature, forming new friendships with children of his own age. A significant moment came when he visited the Sanctuary of Our Lady of Pompeii at the age of five. His Polish babysitter, Beata, a faithful Catholic, who looked after Carlo for four years, recalls his devotion to the Blessed Mother and how he consecrated himself to Our Lady of the Rosary of Pompeii: "He made us take him there to do the special consecration ... and afterwards, all of us together recited the Rosary before the miraculous image of the holy Virgin."

Back in Milan, at the age of seven, Carlo first attended a prestigious school, the Istituto San Carlo. He remained there just three months, before he was transferred to the Istituto Tommaseo, run by the Marcelline Sisters, because it was closer to the Acutis home. There Carlo was educated from January 1998 until September 2005. At the age of fourteen, Carlo moved to secondary school

> The Rosary is the shortest ladder to heaven.

in the rigorous setting of the Jesuit-run Leo XIII Classical Lyceum in Milan. There are testimonies from his Jesuit teachers, staff and classmates of how Carlo thrived in this environment, showing himself to be a generous, affectionate and brilliant young man.

Like any youth growing up, Carlo had his weaknesses and temptations. Not only did he come from a wealthy family, he was also good-looking. He was a natural joker, who enjoyed making his classmates and teachers laugh. His report cards record how he could be disruptive. He realised this and made an effort to change. His brilliance with the internet and computer technology, recognised even by experienced programmers, undoubtedly brought temptations, although no trace of immoral sites was found on his computer after his death. Steve Jobs, co-founder of Apple, was one of his heroes. Carlo often repeated his phrase: "Your time is limited, so don't waste it living someone else's life ... Being the richest man in the cemetery doesn't interest me. Going to bed at night, saying we've done something wonderful, that's what matters to me." He would develop a passion for playing video games, Pokémon and PlayStation, but, with a discerning sense of the risks, he limited himself to doing so for one hour each week, as a penance and a spiritual discipline. Carlo was a lover of life: "From whatever point of view you look, life is always fantastic," he would say. He played sports, loved animals (he had two cats, four dogs, and lots of goldfish!), played the saxophone and had a sweet tooth.

Starting with small struggles, Carlo learned how to master the art of self-control and grow in the virtue of temperance. Putting on weight, for example, made him understand the need for self-control: "What does it matter if you can win a thousand battles, if you cannot defeat your own corrupt passions? The real battle is within ourselves." Purity was important to him. "Each person reflects the light of God," he would often say. So, even with his peers, he defended the Church's teaching on the human body as a gift from God in areas such as sexuality and abortion. When the Acutis family began spending time in Assisi – where Carlo says that he felt "happiest of all" – he was a regular at the town's swimming pool and enjoyed hikes through the Umbrian countryside with the family dogs. In most ways then, Carlo was a very normal boy, born in London, and brought up in Milan, Centola and Assisi.

From whatever point of view you look, life is always fantastic! 99

But there was also something quite different about him. Even at four years of age, Carlo would not pass in front of a Church without asking to enter and blow kisses to Jesus. He would describe the Blessed Mother as "the only woman in my life." As he walked in the park, he collected the most beautiful flowers to place before a statue or image of Our Lady. "Your son is special," many told his mother, including the parish priest, teachers, classmates and even the porter of the house where they lived in Milan. Carlo also read the Bible and biographies of the saints, and asked deep questions about the faith that astonished his mother: "I was perplexed by his devotion. He was so small and so sure. I understood that it was his thing, but that he was also calling me. So, I began my journey of rapprochement to the faith. I followed him."

In past times, it was the parents who transmitted the faith to their children, as per the promises made in Baptism, but, in the Acutis family, the opposite occurred. His mother, moved by Carlo's evident love and interest, spoke to a faith-filled, elderly friend for advice, who pointed her to a holy priest in Bologna, Father Ilio Carrai. He told Antonia to begin studying theology, which she did at the theological faculty in Milan, largely at the weekends when she was able to. According to Nicola Gori, the postulator of Carlo's cause for sainthood, Carlo "managed to drag his relatives, his parents, to Mass every day. It was not the other way around; it was not his parents bringing the little boy to Mass, but it was he who managed to get himself to Mass and to convince others to receive Communion daily." Antonia Acutis admits that because of Carlo's exemplary love for the Eucharist, she started to go to Mass. "This was actually because of Carlo. Carlo for me was a sort of little saviour." He saved her from a life far removed from God.

The most significant moment in Carlo's journey to holiness came when he was seven years old. Even before he had reached the appropriate age, Carlo asked boldly to receive First Holy Communion. Monsignor Pasquale Macchi, the former secretary of Pope St Paul VI, attested that he was ready with his maturity and level of Christian formation. His one request was that Carlo should receive the Eucharist for the first time in silence at the Bernaga de Perego monastery, near Lecco in northern Italy. It was here, on 16th June 1998, before the eyes of cloistered

The Eucharist is truly the Heart of Jesus.

Always to be united with Jesus, this is my programme of life. 99

nuns dedicated to a life of contemplative prayer, that Carlo received, for the first time, Jesus in Holy Communion. The Superior of the Sisters recalls the moment:

Composed and calm during the time of Holy Mass, he began to show signs of "impatience" as the time to receive Holy Communion approached. With Jesus in his heart, after holding his head in his hands, he began to move as if he could no longer sit still. It seemed that something had happened in him, only known to him, something too big that he could not contain. The nuns closest to the altar could not help but look at him with deep emotion, albeit through the thin curtains of the iron grill, and realise that Carlo had quenched the desire of such a great wait. This is why he remained in everyone's heart.

Having received the sacraments of Baptism and Eucharist (he would be confirmed on 24th May 2003), a new phase began in Carlo's relationship with the eucharistic Jesus, which he described as his "highway to heaven." It would become the foundation of his journey to sainthood.

CHAPTER TWO

Carlo's Way to Sanctity: Five Simple Practices

If we wish to be a saint, we first need to desire it. Next, we need constancy. Carlo's dad, Andrea, is a discreet man of few words, but offers essential fatherly advice in this respect:

How many times have we heard the phrase, "Carlo is a special boy." He had a special gift of being liked, but this attitude does not explain the mark he left in so many hearts. In Carlo, one could admire a continuous and ever-renewed orientation towards good. This was possible thanks to his surrender to the Lord. His secrets were a firm and ever renewed willingness to put God first and the constant use of the treasures administered by the Church – the Eucharist and Confession. The result was a harmonious personality, which radiated a great serenity.

Finally, we need a road map. The life and witness of Blessed Carlo Acutis show us the way: "Always to be united with Jesus, this is my programme of life." To live with Jesus, for Jesus and in Jesus is the simple and achievable roadmap that he sets out for us in five practices.

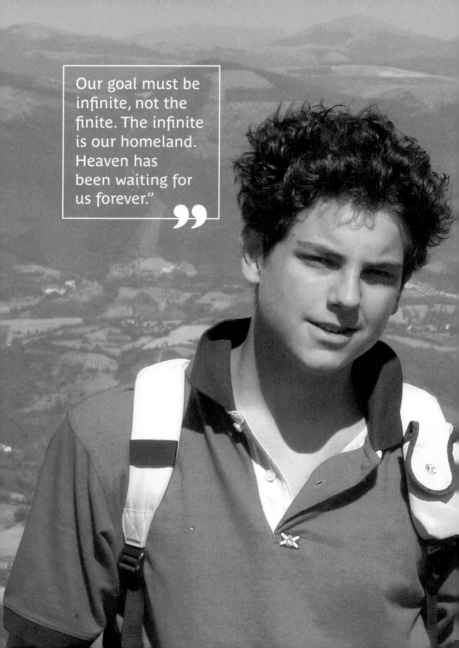

"Our goal must be infinite, not the finite. The infinite is our homeland. Heaven has been waiting for us forever."

1 Frequent Reception of the Eucharist:
The first practice that made him a saint.

Carlo strove to participate in Mass every day. With smiling confidence, he declared, "You go straight to heaven if you participate in the Mass every day."

The reason was simple. The foundation for holiness is a personal and intimate relationship with Jesus. "The more we receive the Eucharist, the more we will become like Jesus, so that on this earth we will have a foretaste of heaven." For Carlo, this relationship was nurtured most especially by his belief in the Real Presence of the Lord in the Eucharist: "Jesus is really present in the world, just as when, in the time of the Apostles, the disciples could see him in flesh and blood walking the streets of Jerusalem." So zealous was Carlo in making known to others the importance of the Eucharist for growing in intimacy with Jesus that he dedicated his computer skills to sharing knowledge of the Real Presence. From the age of eleven, he researched the eucharistic miracles in seventeen countries throughout the world, visiting many of the places where they occurred and cataloguing them on the internet. The website he built comprises 160 pages or "panels". He also created exhibitions of eucharistic miracles that have made the rounds of more than ten thousand parishes worldwide, with exhibitions on all five continents, and in non-Catholic countries such as Russia and China, at

Marian shrines such as Fatima and Guadalupe, and in over a hundred universities in the United States alone. Carlo was a missionary through the internet, such that he is already being called its heavenly patron.

The first practice in becoming a saint is frequent reception of Jesus in the Eucharist. This is what Carlo's brief but intense life teaches us. By receiving Jesus in the Eucharist, we are given divine and eternal life within us. So, for Carlo, the centre and heart of his entire life was to meet Jesus in daily Mass. After receiving his First Holy Communion at the age of seven, his attachment to the Eucharist grew continuously. If he could not receive it for some serious reason, such as sickness, he would do so through spiritual communion. This was a deepening relationship with the best and most faithful of friends. If the family travelled, the first place that Carlo would look for was the nearest church and its Mass times. He was so utterly convinced of the importance of the Mass that, after making his First Holy Communion, he was insistent that his family consecrate itself to the Sacred Heart of Jesus, which it did. His reason is as simple as it is profound: "The Eucharist is truly the Heart of Jesus." He could not understand why sports stadiums were full of people and churches were empty. He repeatedly said, "They have to see, they have to understand."

While taking part in daily Mass he was fully conscious that "with the fruits of the daily Eucharist, souls sanctify

> I like to speak with Jesus about all that I am living and feeling.

themselves in an excellent way and are strengthened especially in dangerous situations that could harm their eternal salvation." The privileged moment to ask the Lord for graces was at the moment of Consecration:

Who can intercede for us more than a God, who offers himself to God? During the Consecration, we need to ask graces of God the Father through the merits of his only begotten Son, Jesus Christ, through his holy wounds, his most precious Blood, and the tears and sorrows of the Virgin Mary, who as his Mother can intercede for us more than anyone else can.

Carlo's simple prayer after receiving communion reveals again how deeply he believed in the divine indwelling of Jesus as a friend: "Jesus, come right in! Make yourself at home!" He was comforted reflecting on the final words left by Jesus as recorded in the Gospel of Matthew: "I will be with you always until the end of time" (*Mt* 28:20). To realise that Carlo was thinking such thoughts, uttering such words and with such intimacy as a young boy is truly astonishing.

A key to understanding Carlo's eucharistic spirituality was his devotion to St John, the beloved disciple of Jesus. At the Last Supper, the young St John leans on the breast of Jesus. He receives the priesthood from Christ with the power to renew the sacrifice of the Cross in the Eucharist: "Do this in memory of me" (*Lk* 22:19). Carlo's commentary on the beloved disciple reveals the invitation and his freedom to accept it, as well as the invitation and freedom of us all:

It's fantastic – like St John, all are called to become beloved disciples. All we need is to become eucharistic souls, adoring souls, allowing God to work those wonders in us, which only he can do. But he wants our will to submit freely. God does not like forcing anyone. He desires our freely-given love.

2 Eucharistic Adoration:
The second practice that made him a saint.

Carlo's relationship with Jesus in the Mass was deepened in Eucharistic Adoration – a short time before and after Mass, and for longer periods when he could.

Among all the saints to whom he was attached, Carlo was attracted most especially by St Francis of Assisi. He longed to spend his summers in Assisi. Conscious of this, Carlo's parents bought a house there in 2001. His mother attests to this love: "Carlo had a special bond with Assisi. He had Assisi in his heart. He said that it was the city where he felt happiest." It should not come as a surprise. The central Italian region of Umbria is steeped in a history of saints and blesseds, not least St Francis and St Clare, the latter often depicted with a monstrance in her hand, bearing the Blessed Sacrament, which she used to ward off the Saracen invaders of Assisi in 1240. Carlo desired to follow in their footsteps, although he joked with his mother that he wanted to be a saint, but not exactly like Francis, "who, as a penance, fasted six months a year!"

Carlo was especially attracted by the devotion of St Francis to the Real Presence of Jesus in the Eucharist, whose prayer of adoration resounds far and wide: "We adore thee, Lord Jesus Christ, who art in all the churches of the whole world." Each day, Carlo tried to visit the tomb of St Francis, to pray to Jesus in the Tabernacle and to the

Poverello, the Poor One of Assisi. Francis, the sometime "party king," who had tasted the fallacy of an opulent, wasted life, was awestruck by God becoming one like us in the Incarnation. Francis's desire to bring to life the birth of Jesus for nearby villagers inspired him to create a live nativity scene in a cave at Greccio. Serving as deacon, and preaching at Mass that Christmas night in 1223, Francis gave eloquent expression to the great humility of God in the Incarnation. But it was especially in the Eucharist that St Francis encountered the descending movement of humility in the Incarnation. He describes his wonder in a letter to the entire Order shortly before his death:

> *Let everyone be struck with fear, let the whole world tremble, and let the heavens exult when Christ, the Son of the living God, is present on the altar in the hands of a priest! O wonderful loftiness and stupendous dignity! O sublime humility! O humble sublimity! The Lord of the universe, God and the Son of God, so humbles himself that for our salvation he hides himself under an ordinary piece of bread! Brothers, look at the humility of God, and pour out your hearts before him! Humble yourselves that you may be exalted by him! Hold back nothing of yourselves for yourselves, that he who gives himself totally to you may receive you totally!*

Carlo Acutis, like Francis, was passionate about the Real Presence of Jesus in the Eucharist. Yet his was not a

> Sadness is the gaze turned towards oneself, happiness is the gaze turned towards God.
> 99

descending, but an ascending movement: "The Eucharist is my highway to heaven." "If we go out in the sun, we get a suntan ... but when we get in front of Jesus in the Eucharist, we become saints." Time spent praying and adoring Jesus in the Blessed Sacrament was meeting Jesus personally:

We can find God, with his Body, his Soul and his Divinity, present in all the tabernacles of the world! If we think about it, we are more fortunate than those who lived two thousand years ago in contact with Jesus, because we have God "really and substantially" present with us always. It's enough to visit the closest church! We have Jerusalem on our doorsteps. Jerusalem is in every church!

Carlo frequently dedicated at least thirty minutes of Eucharistic Adoration to the souls in purgatory to obtain for them a plenary indulgence. He had dreamed once of

his maternal grandfather in purgatory, asking Carlo to pray for him. He was especially attached to the Portiuncula, the small fourth century church where Saint Francis laid the foundations of his Order, now located in the Basilica of St Mary of the Angels. One night in 1216, St Francis was moved to pray there. Jesus and his Blessed Mother appeared to him and asked what he desired. Francis responded, "O God, although I am a great sinner, I beseech you to grant a full pardon of sins to all who, having repented and confessed their sins, shall visit this church." Francis's wish was granted and ratified by Pope Honorius III. The Indulgence exists to this day in the "Great Pardon of Assisi," both for oneself and for souls in purgatory.

For Carlo, his relationship with Jesus was nurtured in extended periods of time praying before the Blessed Sacrament. "I like to speak to Jesus about all that I am living and feeling." Every year, especially during winter, he engaged in spiritual exercises in La Verna, where Saint Francis, in a time of deep personal crisis, had received the sacred stigmata in 1224. On one occasion, Carlo spent six weeks there. In this place of silence, Carlo was able to pray and meditate. Carlo understood that prayer is essential for growing in intimacy with Jesus:

To him I can always confide something, I can also complain, question him about his silence and tell him what I do not understand. And then, within me, I find a word that he sends me: a moment of the Gospel that fills me with conviction and certainty.

Prayer before Jesus brought to maturity within Carlo the desire to give himself unreservedly like Jesus, the Lamb who was slain. His spiritual guide bears witness to the fruits that it bore in this young boy, who so desired to grow in his love for Jesus:

He practised Eucharistic Adoration several times each week and every time that I met him, he told me the advances that he made through it. A short while before he died, I met him at my home in Bologna, and he recounted how he managed to attain such positive results through Eucharistic Adoration. Thanks to it, his love for the Lord increased greatly.

Carlo's friendship with Jesus also grew. Eucharistic Adoration was fundamental in Carlo's journey to be a saint: "By standing before the eucharistic Christ, we become holy." Turning one's gaze towards Jesus was a practice that Carlo followed with constancy. He wrote in his journal:

Sadness is the gaze turned towards oneself, happiness is the gaze turned towards God. Conversion is nothing more than lifting your gaze upwards from low to high: Just a simple movement of the eyes.

3 Spiritual Guide and Regular Confession:
The third practice that made him a saint.

Carlo's desire to be a saint is seen perhaps most clearly in his seeking out a spiritual guide to whom he could confess regularly. It is truly remarkable that Carlo sought out a spiritual father as a young boy. No time is too early or too late! The important point is to find such a person. A spiritual father helps the son or daughter to know the Lord and to fulfil God's will in his or her life. "If only I had had a spiritual director from the beginning," writes St Faustina Kowalska of the Blessed Sacrament, "then I would not have wasted so many of God's graces."

Carlo chose as his spiritual guide Fr. Ilio Carrai, whom his mother had turned to for advice about her own faith. Bologna is a fair distance from Milan and Assisi, yet Carlo willingly travelled there each month. He appears to have known that the path to being a saint requires cooperation with the graces that God sends through the Sacraments, through prayer, and through a constant dying-to-self so as to be perfect in charity. This is God's will. "Only the one who does the will of God will be truly free," Carlo would say.

Carlo's spiritual father recounts how Carlo visited him with constancy. Almost always at the end of their meetings, Carlo asked for the sacrament of Reconciliation, confessing even the smallest faults. "The only thing that we must really fear is sin," he would say. "We need to make the exodus from sin with firmness." He followed his spiritual father's counsel in confessing every week, whether in Milan or Assisi. "Why do people worry so much about the beauty of their own body and not about the beauty of their soul?" he wondered. Fr. Mario Perego, a priest of Carlo's parish church in Milan, Santa Maria Segreta, to whom he confessed regularly, attests to Carlo's desire to seek union with Jesus by confronting the defects that he struggled with, such as gluttony or distractions, when at school or while praying the Rosary:

He was a boy of exceptional transparency, truly limpid. He desired to improve in everything, especially in love for his parents from whom he learned love for the Lord... In order to thank the Lord and feel ever more ready to improve, he received the sacrament of Reconciliation each week, happy to listen to the voice of the Lord.

Carlo also trusted in God's infinite mercy. In his bedroom, he kept an image of the merciful Jesus and a small statue of the Infant Jesus of Prague. He lived through the Great Jubilee of the year 2000, when St John Paul II instituted the Feast of Divine Mercy on the first Sunday of Easter, *Dominica in albis*. He involved his parents in praying the novena of mercy that was given by Jesus to St Faustina Kowalska:

I desire that the Feast of Mercy be a refuge and shelter for all souls, and especially for poor sinners (...). I pour

Without him, I can do nothing.

out a whole ocean of graces upon those souls who approach the fount of my mercy. The soul that will go to confession and receive Holy Communion shall obtain complete forgiveness of sins and punishment; on that day all the divine floodgates through which grace flows are opened. Let no soul fear to draw near to me, even though its sins be as scarlet (Diary, 699).

For Carlo, just as St Francis did in a literal way, holiness involved stripping oneself: "Holiness is not the process of adding, but subtracting: less of me to leave space for God." Carlo uses a metaphor to help us understand why:

In order to rise up high, a hot air balloon needs to shed weight, just like the soul, which, in order to raise itself up to heaven, needs to remove those small weights, called venial sins. If by chance, there is a mortal sin, the soul falls to the ground. Confession is like the fire underneath the balloon, enabling the soul to rise again… It is important to go to confession often, because the soul is very complex.

4 Devotion to Our Blessed Mother and the Saints:
The fourth practice that made him a saint.

Carlo had a very strong devotion to the Blessed Mother and the saints, which began from a very young age. "The Virgin Mother is the only woman in my life ... I never fail to keep the most gracious appointment of the day – recitation of the Holy Rosary."

Carlo felt Mary was close to him, just as he felt close to Jesus in the Eucharist. He was baptised in a church with her name – Our Lady of Dolours – that was dedicated to Our Lady of Fatima. For Carlo, Our Lady loved him as a mother, and he wanted to return that love. As a four-year-old boy, he took flowers to place before her statues or images in churches. He wished his whole family to kneel before the miraculous image of Our Lady of the Rosary at the Sanctuary of Pompeii. At the grotto of Our Lady of Lourdes, he made the promise to be forever faithful to reciting the Rosary. Carlo was especially struck by Our Lady's apparitions in 1917 to the three shepherd children Lucia, Jacinta and Francesco, at the Cova da Iria in Fatima, Portugal. It was one of his last trips in 2006, the year that he died. The children were about the same age as Carlo and he wondered what the words spoken meant for him. The resplendent figure of the Angel of Fatima, who described itself as "The Angel of Peace" against the historical background of the First World War and the

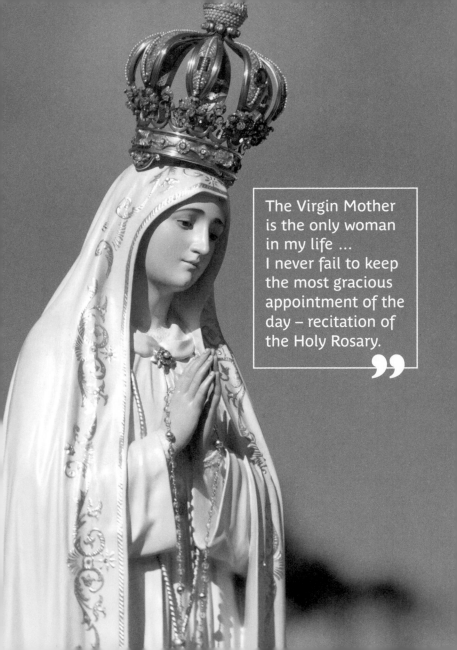

The Virgin Mother is the only woman in my life ... I never fail to keep the most gracious appointment of the day – recitation of the Holy Rosary.

"

emergence of oppressive atheistic regimes, invited these three young children to offer reparation for the offences committed against the Eucharist. Our Lady told them: "Many souls go to hell...there are none to sacrifice and pray for them." Carlo was committed to the call of Our Lady of Fatima, who described herself as "the Lady of the Rosary," to pray the Rosary every day with the prayer she gave on 13th July 1917: "O my Jesus, forgive us our sins, save us from the fires of hell, and lead all souls to heaven, especially those in most need of thy mercy." His prayers and the offering of his sufferings for the Pope were a direct response to the call of Our Lady of Fatima to offer penances and sacrifices for the Supreme Pontiff, whom he refused to criticise.

It was highly significant and providential that Carlo grew up and was formed largely during the Pontificate of St John Paul II, who instituted the Year of the Rosary (2003-2004) and that of the Eucharist (2004-2005). For Carlo, the Eucharist and the Virgin Mary were two pillars on which every Christian needs to build his or her life. Moreover, one cannot help but think that Carlo's "programme of life" – "Always united to Jesus" – was inspired by the motto that St John Paul II had taken for his pontificate, *Totus tuus*, which comes from the teaching of St Louis Marie de Montfort: "I am all yours and all I have is yours, O dear Jesus, through Mary, your holy Mother."

We have already noted how Carlo found inspiration in the saints – Francis, Clare, John the Apostle. Alongside reading from the Scriptures each day, he also researched the lives of the saints. He created several websites on the topic, one dedicated especially to young saints. He had a keen interest in those who were able to achieve holiness quickly. The website even included a section on how many friends we have in heaven. Carlo wanted friends in heaven!

He admired St Anthony of Padua for his eucharistic piety and for being a true missionary. He was struck by St Paul's zeal to preach the Gospel, even to the point of martyrdom. Carlo was moved by the tireless activity of St John Bosco, visiting his rooms in Turin on different occasions. His words left a mark on Carlo: "Idleness, the Holy Spirit tells us, is the father of all vices. Keeping occupied fights it and conquers everything." The sacrifices made by the three shepherd children of Fatima, similar in age to him, in answer to Our Lady's call for conversion, penance and prayer, were an example to him. He meditated on the words spoken by Our Lady in 1858 to St Bernadette Soubirous in the grotto of Massabielle, Lourdes: "I do not promise to make you happy in this world, but in the next." Ultimately, he made his own the phrase of Sacred Scripture that motivated St Francis Xavier to bring Jesus to the farthest corners of the world: "What does it profit a man if he gains the whole world and loses himself?" (*Lk* 9:25).

Again, the source of Carlo's devotion to the Virgin Mary and the saints was rooted in the Eucharist. His friend Rajesh recalls:

"Once he also spoke to me about devotion to the practice of offering the First Fridays of the month to the Immaculate Heart of Mary. He said: "The heart of Jesus and the heart of Mary are linked indissolubly and when we receive Communion, we are in direct contact with Our Lady and the saints in heaven. God is very happy when souls draw close frequently to his great gifts of the Eucharist and Confession".

The Blessed Mother and the saints walked by Carlo's side, not replacing his personal traits and skills, but elevating them to live well with Jesus, for Jesus, in Jesus: "God has written for each one of us a unique and unrepeatable story, but he has left us the freedom to write the ending."

5 Charity:
The fifth practice that made him a saint.

To be a saint, Carlo said that we need to love: "A life will be really beautiful if we come to love God above all things and our neighbour as ourselves." Carlo loved. "Everything passes away… the only thing that will make us truly beautiful in God's eyes is the way that we have loved him and our brothers."

From a very young age, Carlo showed himself to be generous in self-giving. "Every person was important for Carlo," his mother says. "In each one he saw the face of Jesus." So he would befriend everyone, including the gatekeepers, janitors, immigrants, and domestic workers in the neighbourhood. He told everyone about the love of Christ. This was especially the case for the marginalised, rejected and weakest. With savings from his pocket money, he bought sleeping bags for the homeless. He brought hot drinks to beggars. He organised fairs in his parish to raise funds for the missions. He spent time volunteering at a soup kitchen run by the Capuchins and Mother Teresa of Calcutta's Missionaries of Charity, in via le Piave, Milan. He gave his savings to enable 2500 meals to be given out to the poor there each day through the *Opera di San Francesco*. "Money," Carlo would say "is nothing more than shredded paper. What counts in life is the nobility of the soul, that is, the way we love God and neighbour."

Carlo offered not only material goods. He gave his very self in establishing a relationship with the "rejects" of society. The testimonies from beggars close to the churches where Carlo attended daily Mass are especially moving. They remember not only Carlo's generosity, but perhaps even more his kindness. One notes: "He was too good and pure for this earth. I shall never forget him." On the day of his funeral, another held up a sign: "The boy died young because he was dear to heaven!" In the poor, Carlo saw God's beloved. In this, he followed the example of St Francis, as recounted by St Bonaventure in his *Legenda Maior*: "He felt his heart melt in the presence of the poor and the sick, and when he could not offer material help, he offered his affection" (8,5).

His charity was most often hidden and worked through small acts: something as simple as choosing freely to have one fewer pairs of shoes or changes of clothes, so that he could perform an extra work of charity with the unspent money. Sheela, who came to do the ironing in the Acutis household, also benefitted from Carlo's charity. On Sundays, Carlo secretly helped her to finish her work, so that she could return home earlier to be with her family.

Carlo's love for the weak and vulnerable extended to children at his school who were bullied, especially those who were disabled in some way. When a friend's parents were in the throes of a bitter divorce, he made a special effort to bring his suffering companion into his own family.

A life will be really beautiful if we come to love God above all things and our neighbour as ourselves.

Rajesh, the Hindu man who worked in the Acutis home from when Carlo was four years old, would accompany Carlo everywhere – school, church, friends' homes, catechism, and on rounds in the neighbourhood to feed the homeless and hungry. Carlo called Rajesh, "My faithful friend." It was Carlo's witness that was the seed of Rajesh's conversion:

He told me that I would be happier if I approached Jesus. I chose to be baptised a Christian because it was he who so affected me with such a deep faith, his charity, and his purity. I have always considered it out of the ordinary because a boy so young, so handsome, and so rich normally prefers a different kind of life.

Sister Giovanna Negrotto still remembers to this day how the young Carlo took such a keen interest in her missionary work in India, insisting on seeing photos of what he called her "great leper friends." The last question that Carlo asked her left her pondering: "What do you think? Is God more pleased with a service like this, generous and tireless, to the least ones of this world, or with prayer?" Upon hearing from Carlo's parents of his untimely death, and how he had offered up his suffering for the Pope and the Church, she realised that Carlo had lived the answer to his question: "Service, yes. Prayer, yes. But no one has greater love than to lay down one's life for one's friends."

The source of Carlo's charity to the end was Jesus in the Eucharist: "Without him, I can do nothing." He knew that God, who is love (*1 Jn* 4;16), created us to love him and our neighbour. To love God means to love my neighbour; one implies the other. So, grasping the extent of God's love for us in the Eucharist – God, who lets himself be so moved by man's situation that he becomes body given, and blood poured out, in Jesus – Carlo was himself drawn into the very dynamic of divine self-giving. He accepted the invitation to love, to the point of offering up his sufferings on his deathbed for others, in response to the gift of God's love in Jesus. He understood well that charity to the end means sacrifice and perseverance: "Life is a gift. As long as we are upon this planet, we can increase our level of charity. The greater it is, the more we shall enjoy the eternal beatitude of God." Nicola Gori, the Postulator of Carlo's cause, testifies:

Carlo passed through tribulation, but his gaze never turned in on himself. He knew how to reach out to others, to come out of his own "I" and put God's will before his own. For this reason, his exit from this world was natural and serene; he knew it meant a definitive meeting with Christ, his Lord with whom he had forged an indissoluble friendship.

Carlo also had an innate sense of the shortness of life, as the Psalm teaches: "Teach us to number our days aright, that we may gain a wisdom of heart" (*Ps* 90;12). He was convinced that he would not grow old. "I shall die young," he often repeated. For him, "every minute that passes is one minute less to sanctify ourselves." Time could not be wasted in those things that "do not please God." This, too, is a reason why Carlo filled his days spending himself – teaching younger children the catechism, feeding the poor, spending time with children at the parish oratory, achieving excellent grades at school, playing the saxophone, designing websites and films – all because he kept a constant union with God in the midst of an extremely busy day.

On his deathbed, the philosopher Søren Kierkegaard said: "The point is to arrive as close to God as possible." Close union with God was what makes Carlo Acutis a saint today, in five simple and constant practices, possible for us all: frequent reception of the Eucharist; Eucharist

Adoration; the guidance of a spiritual father and regular Confession; entrusting oneself to the Blessed Mother and the inspiration of the saints; and acts of charity, however small or great. "The point is to arrive as close to God as possible." Or, as Blessed Carlo put it: "Not I, but God."

CHAPTER THREE

Carlo's Witness to the End and Beyond

A story is told about the dying days of St Francis of Assisi. At the bishop's residence in Assisi, next to where the body of Carlo Acutis now lies in the Sanctuary of the Renunciation, Francis spent several days before being taken to the Portiuncula, sick, exhausted, his eyes almost blind, and his limbs full of pain. Yet the home resounded with the song of the praises of God in Francis's "Canticle to Brother Sun." This surprised many. How could the saintly Francis be singing when he was facing the dark spectre of death so young, just forty-four years of age, leaving behind all that he had begun? Francis almost had to justify himself to his Minister General, Brother Elia. "Am I preparing myself to die? But of course! It's precisely for that reason that I'm singing the praises of the Lord." For he who became totally one with Christ, "sister death" became "sister life." Francis was able to die with a song in his heart.

In September 2006, at the end of his summer holiday in Assisi, Carlo went, as was his custom, to pray at the tomb of St Francis, to seek the saint's intercession for the year ahead. Strangely, the basilica was closed, when it was normally open. In what was to follow, he would read that as a sign. St Francis was waiting for him in heaven.

In early October 2006, illness struck. At first, it seemed to be a flu that his classmates had also contracted. His slightly swollen lymph nodes, however, pointed to something more serious. A few days later, Carlo noticed blood in his urine. His weight suddenly increased. From his bed, he told his parents: "I offer what I will have to suffer to the Lord for the Pope and for the Church, to skip purgatory and go straight to heaven." It is also said that Carlo was offering his sufferings for an end to the burgeoning scandal of paedophilia in the United States.

The fever did not leave him, and he grew weaker. He was taken first to the paediatric Clinica de Marchi, in via della Commenda, Milan. As soon as he arrived there, the medics realised how serious his condition was. He was diagnosed with one of the worst and most aggressive forms of leukaemia – acute promyelocytic leukaemia – which destroys red blood cells quicker than the body produces them. His parents, and then Carlo, were informed of the gravity of his condition. When left alone in the room, he told his parents, "The Lord has sent me a wake-up call."

He was transferred to the hospital of San Gerardo in Monza. Crossing the threshold of the hospital, Carlo said to his mother: "I'm not getting out of here." His mother and grandmother remained by his bedside. When a doctor asked him if he was in great pain, he responded: "There are others suffering much more than me." His swelling increased. On 11th October at 2.30pm, he entered into a coma from a brain haemorrhage caused by the leukaemia. His heart stopped beating at 6.45am in the morning on 12th October 2006, the liturgical memorial of the Virgin of Pilar and Our Lady of Aparecida, and the eve of the last apparition of Our Lady in Fatima. With his sense of living life to the full and embracing the happiness of death as the gateway to heaven, Carlo Acutis died with a radiant smile on his face, transfigured by the eucharistic light of Jesus, and offering his sufferings for the Pope and for the Church. He was just fifteen years old.

His body was taken home and the coffin left open for three days. Soon the room was filled with classmates and others who came to venerate their friend. On 14th October, Carlo's funeral was celebrated in his parish church, Santa Maria Segreta in Milan. It was filled to overflowing. His mother describes the scene: "I have never seen people like this before." People recounted to Antonia stories about what Carlo had done which she had never heard. Most who were there were unknown to Carlo's parents. Many were immigrants and beggars. The mood was festive with the bells ringing for the Angelus. It seemed as if Carlo had been received into heaven. His burial followed in the family tomb in Ternengo (Biella), before his remains were transferred to the cemetery of Assisi, as had been his wish, in 2007.

As throughout his life, Carlo offered a testimony of faith in his dying days. His mother, Antonia, recalls how he approached his suffering and death. Carlo would try not to complain, but rather to smile. "Death is the start of new life," he would say. Towards the end, he was too weak to move himself. He worried for the nurses who had to lift him, that he was too heavy for them. Before he died, he said: "Mama, I will give you signs, that I am with God." Clearly, Carlo was ready for heaven.

Carlo's understanding of suffering was rooted in the Cross. His mother recalls what Carlo said from his deathbed: "Golgotha is for everyone. No one escapes the cross." Carlo had been a witness to many in his lifetime, and now his dying days became a powerful, life-changing testimony for his mother: "He convinced me of this," she says. "If I am a good Catholic, how can I be afraid of this?"

God, not his own condition, was the focus of Carlo's attention. This was his secret: God was the single goal and objective of his short life: "Sadness is looking at ourselves, happiness is looking towards God." And so: "Our goal must be infinite, not the finite. The infinite is our homeland. Heaven has been waiting for us forever." This helps to explain why, in his real bodily suffering, he was not afraid of dying. "Do not be afraid because, with the incarnation of Jesus, death becomes life, and there's no need to escape: in eternal life something extraordinary awaits us." Carlo teaches us to look at death through the eyes of faith. He taught this to his mother. Without faith, she says, she would have remained inconsolable after the death of her young son. With faith, her mourning can turn to hope.

Others also witnessed to Carlo's saintly death. The hospital chaplain, Father Sandro Villa, who administered the Anointing of the Sick and Holy Communion on 10th October 2006, the day before Carlo fell into a coma, recalls the witness of Carlo even as he suffered:

I found myself in front of a boy. His pale yet serene face surprised me. It was unthinkable in a seriously ill person, let alone an adolescent. I was also amazed by the composure and devotion with which he received the two sacraments. It was difficult for him, but he seemed to have been waiting for them and needed them.

The now elderly Father Villa has a challenging word for priests, too: "If only we could celebrate Mass with the same faith as Carlo." Two doctors who treated Carlo, Dr Andrea Biondi and Dr Mòmcilo Jankovic, were also moved:

His faith in God, which he had also wished and still wished to transmit to others, to his neighbour, shone through him. He taught us a great deal: life, whether short or long, must be lived intensely for oneself, but also and above all for others.

Carlo died with a 'reputation' for sanctity. The newly named Prefect of the Congregation for the Causes of Saints, Marcello Cardinal Semeraro, made it a point to entrust his new mission to the young Blessed Carlo by visiting Assisi to close Blessed Carlo's tomb on 19th October 2020.

In the Congregation, there is amazement at the great stream of interest in Carlo. For beatification and canonisation, there is a clause that requires the "fame" of sanctity. Carlo did not need it, and does not need it. The Book of Wisdom tells us, "Having become perfect in a short while, he reached the fulness of a long life" (Ws 4:13).

Because Carlo had reached so many in his lifetime – through his international exhibitions and internet ministry – thousands of letters and emails came to his family. The Mayor of Assisi, Stefania Proietti, recalls how, soon after Carlo's remains were transferred to the cemetery in Assisi, her grandmother took her to Carlo's grave to seek his intercession.

How soon afterwards the process began for raising him to the altars tells us of Carlo's witness of holiness in life and in death. Normally, it cannot begin until five years after death. This waiting period is to ascertain that the person has an enduring reputation for sanctity among the faithful. On 12th October 2012, just six years to the day after his death, the Archdiocese of Milan, where Carlo died, opened the Cause for his canonisation. The necessary granting of the *nulla osta* (declaration that there is no impediment) from the Congregation for the Causes of Saints arrived on the feast day of Our Lady of Fatima, 13th May 2013. With this formal act, Carlo was declared "Servant of God." In this phase established by the diocese, and known as "postulation," the Cause gathered testimony about the life and virtues of the Servant of God, Carlo Acutis.

This documentary phase concluded on 24th November 2016. The results, along with the bound volumes of documentation, or *Acta* (Acts), were communicated to the Congregation for the Causes of the Saints.

On 5th July 2018, following an audience granted to Angelo Cardinal Amato, then Prefect of the Congregation for the Causes of Saints, Pope Francis signed a decree advancing Carlo's cause to "Venerable" and thus recognising his heroic virtues. By then the Holy Father already knew of Carlo and spoke specifically of his life message in his Post-Synodal Apostolic Exhortation, *Christus vivit*:

He saw that many young people, wanting to be different, really end up being like everyone else, running after whatever the powerful set before them with the mechanisms of consumerism and distraction. In this way they do not bring forth the gifts the Lord has given them; they do not offer the world those unique personal talents that God has given to each of them. As a result, Carlo said, "everyone is born as an original, but many people end up dying as photocopies." Don't let that happen to you! (n.106).

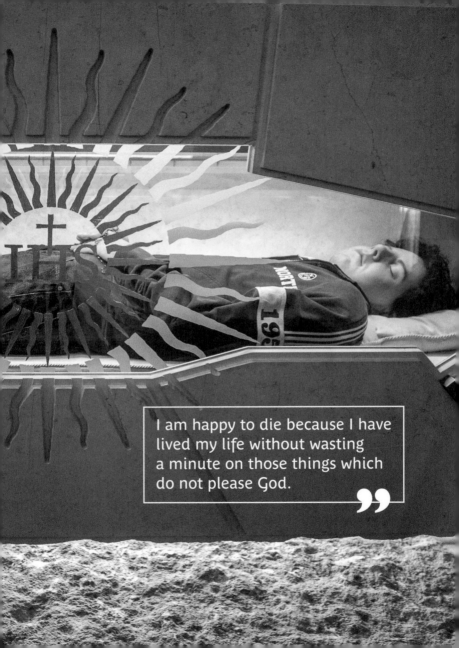

I am happy to die because I have lived my life without wasting a minute on those things which do not please God.

99

As part of the process for the cause of canonisation, the body of Carlo was exhumed in the ceremony of the *elevatio* for the recognition of his mortal remains on 23rd January 2019. The same day, the coffin was taken from the cemetery of Assisi first to the Capuchin Convent in via San Francesco for treatment of the corpse. On 5th April 2019, Carlo's body was carried first to the lower Basilica of Saint Francis, and then with a stop at the Basilica of Saint Clare, taken to the Cathedral of San Rufino. The Bishops of Umbria celebrated Mass at the Cathedral around the body and a vigil was held that night, presided by the auxiliary Bishop of Milan, Monsignor Paolo Martinelli, OFM Cap. The next day, 6th April 2019, the body was transferred in solemn procession to the Shrine of Renunciation – the former Cathedral also known as the parish of Saint Mary Major – of the Diocese of Assisi. Blessed Carlo Acutis lies there today in the Sanctuary's right nave in a magnificent rose-coloured tomb, surrounded by white marble with scenes from his life and some of his sayings, elevated from the ground to show that the Eucharist has raised him to heaven. It is fitting that his final resting place is next to the very room in the Bishop's house where the young Francis stripped himself naked, turned away from his worldly inheritance and surrendered himself to our Father in heaven.

On 16th November 2019, the medical council of the Congregation for the Causes of Saints expressed a positive opinion on an alleged miracle attributed to Carlo. The miracle regarded the healing of a gravely ill young boy, named Mattheus, in Brazil. Father Marcelo Tenorio, the parish priest of San Sebastiano, where the miracle took place, had learned of Carlo Acutis some years previously. He immediately began to spread news about Carlo, creating the Brazilian apostolate "Carlo Acutis: The Angel of Youth." On one of his pilgrimages to Assisi, Father Marcelo gave Carlo's father an image of Our Lady of Aparecida, so that it could be placed in his son's room in Milan.

I asked the Blessed Mother that the miracle for his beatification would take place here in Brazil. I believed that placing her image in Carlo's room would assure this. And what a surprise! Not only did the miracle happen in Brazil, it happened right here in our parish of San Sebastiano.

It also happened on the very anniversary of the day that Carlo had left this world to enter eternal life. Father Marcelo had obtained a relic from Carlo's mother, and invited parishioners to a Mass and prayer service to beg for Carlo's intercession for any healing that they might need. Here is what transpired in Father Marcelo's words:

On 12th October 2013, in our parish, at the moment of blessing with the relic of Carlo Acutis in the chapel of Our Lady of Aparecida, accompanied by his grandfather, a child came forward who suffered from annular pancreas, a very serious congenital disease that can be

*fatal. The disease made the boy vomit continually, and
so he became weaker and weaker – his body rejected
everything that he ate, even liquids. He came to church
with a towel because his condition was obviously very
serious. This affliction made him weaker and weaker,
and the little boy was surely going to die.*

When they got in line to receive the blessing, the boy,
barely four years old and weighing just twenty pounds,
asked his grandfather what sort of grace he should ask
for. "Ask to stop vomiting," his grandfather immediately
replied. And, so, he did. When it was his turn, the boy
touched the reliquary holding Carlo's relic and said in a firm
voice, "I wish I could stop vomiting so much!" Nicola Gori,
the Postulator of Carlo's cause, attests: "Healing began
immediately, to the point that the physiology of the organ
in question changed." On his way home from Mass, four-
year-old Mattheus told his mother, Luciana Vianna, that
he had been cured. Once at home, he asked for chips,
rice, beans and steak, which were his brothers' favourite
foods. Until then, he had been on an all-liquid diet. He
ate everything without vomiting and has never done so
again. Following this, Mattheus's family had him undergo
medical tests, which demonstrated his complete healing.
His physicians were mystified by what had happened.

Following an affirmative vote by the scientific and
theological commissions, and then the members of the

Congregation for the Causes of Saints, on 21st February 2020, in a meeting with Angelo Cardinal Becciù, then Prefect of the Congregation for the Causes of Saints, the Vatican announced that Pope Francis had formally recognised the healing of Mattheus as a miracle, attributed to the intercession of Venerable Carlo Acutis. The Supreme Pontiff authorised the promulgation of the decree regarding "the miracle attributed to the intercession of the Venerable Servant of God Carlo Acutis, layperson; born in London, England on 3rd May 1991, and died in Monza, Italy on 12th October 2006." The door was thus opened to the beatification in the Upper Basilica of Saint Francis, Assisi, at 4:30 pm on 10th October 2020. The long-awaited joy finally had a date.

Carlo's beatification Mass, celebrated by the papal legate, Agostino Cardinal Vallini, and bishops and priests from Umbria and beyond, took place while the clouds of the coronavirus pandemic continued to darken the horizons of millions throughout the entire world. In the seven days leading up to the beatification, and in the nine days after, even with all the travel and other restrictions in place, some forty thousand people are said to have filed past Carlo's glass tomb, opened by the Archbishop-Bishop of Assisi, Domenico Sorrentino on 1st October 2020. There Carlo lay in jeans and a pair of Nikes, his own casual clothes that he preferred in life. The Archbishop said:

I open his tomb for these weeks so that his body, arranged with art and love, may be viewed by those who feel connected to his figure, attracted by his example and eager for his intercession. In some way, his earthly face will be seen again. But that face – lest we forget – no longer points to itself, but to God.

In the beatification ceremony, Carlo's parents carried a relic of their son's heart, which will be made available for pilgrimages. Carlo's brother and sister, Michele and Francesca, twins conceived four years after Carlo's death and then just ten years old, were present too. Few were allowed inside the basilica because of the pandemic restrictions, but countless others, perhaps millions, followed the beatification in the piazzas of Assisi and throughout the world. His beatification was a ray of much needed light for those struggling with the consequences of the pandemic, with health challenges, like little Mattheus, and with socio-economic difficulties. In his homily, Cardinal Vallini proclaimed Carlo's beatification as "good news, a powerful proclamation that a youth of our times, someone like many of us, has been conquered by Christ and has become a radiant light for those who want to know him and follow his example. It's up to us now to follow him."

Yet Carlo was not only a youth of our time. Carlo, a computer wizard, was ahead of his time. He catalogued the world's eucharistic miracles and made them available through the internet to make Jesus known. In the months of lockdown due to the coronavirus pandemic, the ensuing solitude and distancing for every stratum of society were alleviated in many ways by connection to Jesus and to neighbour through the internet, including the celebration of Mass and other liturgical moments. Carlo, this saintly teenager of our age and possible patron saint of the internet, aids us in the love of God and of our neighbour through his intercession – in a way, his "programming" – from heaven.

Carlo's aim was simple. In his short life, he used his talents and skills for the greater glory of God and to bring souls to Jesus and heaven: "Not I, but God." Carlo Acutis indeed died not as a photocopy, but an original.

By standing before the Eucharist, we become holy.

Closing Reflections

The proclamation of Carlo Acutis as Blessed means that he can also be venerated in the liturgy of the Church. In the Opening Prayer for the Mass in his memory – to be celebrated each year on 12th October – as set by the Congregation for Divine Worship and the Discipline of the Sacraments, we read:

> O God, who in the life of Blessed Carlo has revealed the unfathomable riches of the Eucharist and made him an example to young people and a witness of mercy to the poor, grant also to us, through his intercession, to live always united to you and to recognise you in our brothers whom we meet along our way.

The prayer is a fitting summary of Carlo's path to becoming a saint. It compels us, and especially the young, to ask God, through his witness and intercession, to make us saints ourselves. We hear in the prayer that God revealed to Carlo the "unfathomable riches of the Eucharist." Then he "made him an example to young people" and "a witness of mercy to the poor." Finally, on the basis of this, the prayer invites us to ask the Lord for two things: one is to "live always united to God," and the other to "recognise you in our brothers whom we meet along our way."

This booklet has described how a young "millennial," born in London in 1991 and who died in Milan in 2006, lived each of these characteristics in his short but intense fifteen years on this earth. More than anything else, Blessed Carlo Acutis, like St Francis of Assisi, was awestruck and energised by the Eucharist. Carlo's life proclaims that each time we receive the Eucharist, and whenever we pause in adoration before the Blessed Sacrament, we do not have before us a mere symbol or fictitious re-enactment of Jesus; rather, it is Jesus himself who is present. And we can meet him, as Carlo liked to point out, as if we were with him on the streets of Jerusalem. In fact even more so, because in his eucharistic presence Jesus does not limit himself to being seen, heard or touched, but makes himself our food, "living bread," upon which we can feed and so become like him. Like the Blessed Mother and the saints, our communion with Jesus, fed through the Eucharist, guided by a spiritual father and purified by the confession of our sins, exemplified by the Blessed Mother and the saints, and nurtured by our charity, unites us to Jesus, so that we remain in him and he in us. What will heaven be after our death if not an abiding in him, in the glory of the Trinity, and in the joy of the angels and saints? It is the promise of a future that invites us to live our present well, as Carlo tells us: "If we only knew what eternity is, we would do everything to change the course of our lives … To love what awaits us tomorrow is to give today the best of our fruit."

For this very reason, Carlo did not find it difficult to be a completely "normal" young man in his way of relating to the things of this world – from sport, to nature, to music, to the gifts of new technologies. His *constancy* in his spiritual practices resulted in an authentic, harmonious personality, which, as his father testifies, "radiated a great serenity." We can be "normal" and a saint, while keeping all that is unique to us as individuals. Through God and with God, Blessed Carlo teaches us that we lose nothing when our life project is to be "always united to Jesus." Instead we gain everything, the great, creative immensity of the freedom of goodness.

Ultimately, Carlo stands before us, as a boy of our times, and says to us: "Have the courage to dare with God! Dare to be a saint!" "You, too, can be a saint," he told his friends. "But you need to want it with all your heart, and, if you do not yet desire it, ask the Lord for it with insistence." Now a Blessed, Carlo has left us a road map: "Act like me," he says, "and you will see the results!"

May I invite you to join me "to act like Carlo," and bring others, too – your friends, children, those you teach or catechise, those far away from the Church – into the journey to be a saint in five simple and constant practices?

- Frequent reception of the Eucharist
- Eucharistic Adoration
- Guidance of a spiritual father and regular Confession
- Devotion to the Blessed Mother through recitation of the Rosary and discovering the lives of the saints
- Acts of charity, small or large

This invitation comes with the certainty that the desire of Blessed Carlo Acutis, as expressed in his own words, will be fulfilled in those who read this book and follow Carlo's five practices:

"You, too, can be a saint. But you need to want it with your whole heart, and, if you do not yet desire it, ask the Lord for it with insistence."

If we go out in the sun,
we get a suntan ... but
when we get in front of
Jesus in the Eucharist,
we become saints.

Sayings of Blessed Carlo Acutis

Present Day Life

"Not I, but God."

"Not love of self, but the glory of God."

"The essential is invisible to the eyes."

"Everyone is born as an original, but many people end up dying as photocopies."

"From whatever point of view you look, life is always fantastic!"

"What does it matter if you can win a thousand battles, if you cannot defeat your own corrupt passions? The real battle is within ourselves."

"Each person reflects the light of God."

"Always to be united with Jesus, this is my programme of life."

"They have to see, they have to understand."

"Only the one who does the will of God will be truly free."

"Without him, I can do nothing."

"Act like me and you will see the results."

Suffering, Death and Eternal Life

"I am happy to die because I have lived my life without wasting a minute on those things which do not please God."

"I shall die young. Every minute that passes is one minute less to sanctify ourselves."

"I offer what I will have to suffer to the Lord for the Pope and for the Church, to skip purgatory and go straight to heaven."

"The Lord has sent me a wake-up call."

"There are others suffering much more than me."

"Death is the start of new life."

"Mama, I will give you signs, that I am with God."

"Golgotha is for everyone. No one escapes the cross."

"Our goal must be infinite, not the finite. The infinite is our homeland. Heaven has been waiting for us forever."

"Do not be afraid because, with the incarnation of Jesus, death becomes life, and there's no need to escape: in eternal life something extraordinary awaits us."

"If we only knew what eternity is, we would do everything to change the course of our lives...To love what awaits us tomorrow is to give today the best of our fruit."

Frequent Reception of the Eucharist

"The Eucharist is my highway to heaven."

"Try to go to Mass every day and to receive Holy Communion."

"You go straight to heaven if you participate in the Mass every day!"

"The more we receive the Eucharist, the more we will become like Jesus, so that on this earth we will have a foretaste of heaven."

"Jesus is really present in the world, just as when, in the time of the Apostles, the disciples could see him in flesh and blood walking the streets of Jerusalem."

"The Eucharist is truly the Heart of Jesus."

"With the fruits of daily Eucharist, souls sanctify themselves in an excellent way and are strengthened especially in dangerous situations that could harm their eternal salvation."

"Who can intercede for us more than a God, who offers himself to God? During the Consecration, we need to ask graces of God the Father through the merits of his only begotten Son, Jesus Christ, through his holy wounds, his most precious Blood, and the tears and sorrows of the Virgin Mary, who as his Mother can intercede for us more than anyone else can."

"Jesus, come right in! Make yourself at home!"

"Like St John, all are called to become beloved disciples. All we need is to become eucharistic souls, adoring souls,

allowing God to work those wonders in us, which only he can do. But he wants our will to submit freely. God does not like forcing anyone. He desires our freely-given love."

Eucharistic Adoration

"If we go out in the sun, we get a suntan ... but when we get in front of Jesus in the Eucharist, we become saints."

"By standing before the Eucharist, we become holy."

"We can find God, with his Body, his Soul and his Divinity, present in all the tabernacles of the world! If we think about it, we are more fortunate than those who lived two thousand years ago in contact with Jesus, because we have God 'really and substantially' present with us always. It's enough to visit the closest church! We have Jerusalem on our doorsteps. Jerusalem is in every church!"

"I like to speak with Jesus about all that I am living and feeling."

"To him I can always confide something, I can also complain, question him about his silence and tell him what I do not understand. And then, within me, I find a word that he sends me: a moment of the Gospel that fills me with conviction and certainty."

"Sadness is the gaze turned towards oneself, happiness is the gaze turned towards God. Conversion is nothing more than lifting your gaze upwards from low to high. Just a simple movement of the eyes."

Guidance of a Spiritual Father and Regular Confession

"We need to work firmly on our exodus from sin."

"The only thing that we must really fear is sin."

"If you can, confess each week, even your venial sins."

"Why do people worry so much about the beauty of their own body and not about the beauty of their soul?"

"In order to rise up high, a hot air balloon needs to shed weight, just like the soul, which, in order to raise itself up to heaven, needs to remove those small weights called venial sins. If by chance there is a mortal sin, the soul falls to the ground. Confession is like the fire underneath the balloon, enabling the soul to rise again … It is important to go to confession often, because the soul is very complex."

Devotion to Our Blessed Mother and the Saints

"You, too, can be a saint. But you need to want it with your whole heart, and, if you do not yet desire it, ask the Lord for it with insistence."

"Holiness is not the process of adding, but subtracting: less of me to leave space for God."

"The only thing we have to ask God for in prayer is the desire to be holy."

"The Virgin Mother is the only woman in my life … I never fail to keep the most gracious appointment of the day – recitation of the Holy Rosary."

"The Rosary is the shortest ladder to heaven."

"The heart of Jesus and the heart of Mary are linked indissolubly and when we receive Communion we are in direct contact with Our Lady and the saints in Paradise. God is very happy when souls draw close frequently to his great gifts of the Eucharist and Confession."

"God has written for each one of us a unique and unrepeatable story, but he has left us the freedom to write the ending."

Charity

"A life will be really beautiful if we come to love God above all things and our neighbour as ourselves."

"Everything passes away … What alone will truly make us beautiful in God's eyes is the way that we have loved him and our brothers."

"Money is nothing more than shredded paper. What counts in life is the nobility of the soul, that is, the way we love God and neighbour."

"What do you think? Is God more pleased with a service like this, generous and tireless, to the least ones of this world, or with prayer?"

"Life is a gift. As long as we are upon this planet, we can increase our level of charity. The greater it is, the more we shall enjoy the eternal beatitude of God."

"O God make me productive grain, efficient grain, effective grain. Jesus, make me a grain of wheat so that I can reach your eucharistic reality, by which I really and truly live."

(Prayer of Blessed Carlo Acutis)

PRAYER TO BLESSED CARLO ACUTIS

O God our Father,
we thank you for giving us Carlo,
a model of life for young people,
and a message of love for all.
You made him fall in love with your son Jesus,
making the Eucharist his "highway to heaven."
You gave him Mary as a beloved mother,
and you made him, through the Rosary,
a cantor of her tenderness.
Receive his prayer for us.
Look above all upon the poor, whom he loved
and assisted.
Grant me too, through his intercession, the grace
that I need (*mention your intention*).
And make our joy full, raising Carlo among
the saints of your Church,
so that his smile shines again for us
to the glory of your name.
Amen.

Our Father, Hail Mary, Glory be.

Imprimatur ✠ Domenico Sorrentino
Bishop of Assisi-Nocera Umbra-Gualdo Tadino

BIBLIOGRAPHY

Gori, Nicola, *Un Genio dell'Informatica in Cielo. Biografia del Servo di Dio Carlo Acutis* (Città del Vaticano, Libreria Editrice Vaticana, 2016).

Occhetta, Francesco, *Carlo Acutis. La Vita oltre il Confine* (Gorle, Bg, Editrice Velar, 2013).

Paris, Giancarlo, *Carlo Acutis. Il Discepolo Prediletto* (Padova, Edizioni Messaggero Padova, 2018).

Sorrentino, Domenico, *Original, Not Photocopies. Carlo Acutis and Francis of Assisi* (Phoenix, AZ, Tau Publishing, LLC, 2020).

IMAGE CREDITS